How Does Your *Garden Grow?*

Written and compiled by Beverly Rose Hopper

Published by
Walrus Productions

Published by Walrus Productions
4805 NE 106th St, Seattle, Washington, 98125
Cover and illustrations by Kathleen Russell
Typography by Steve Norman of The Durland Group

Printed by Vaughan Printing, Nashville, Tennessee

Hopper, Beverly Rose
    How Does Your Garden Grow? / Beverly Rose Hopper. -- 1st ed.
    p. cm.
    ISBN 0-9635176-8-6

    1. Gardening--Humor. 2. Gardening--Quotations, maxims, etc.
I. Title.

SB455.H66 1995   635
                                          QBI94-21163

Printed in the United States of America
10 9 8 7 6 5 4 3 2

INTRODUCTION

How Does Your Garden Grow? is a whimsical collection reflecting the true spirit of gardening. It embodies the inspiration, creation, laughter, and hope that we find within our gardens and ourselves.

ACKNOWLEDGMENTS

Thank you to my husband Martin for his support and understanding, especially in regard to the other love of my life – my garden. To my children Neil and Emily Rose who are learning to love to garden as much as I do. To my mother and father for instilling in me "good gardening genes."

I would also like to thank my publishers Kathleen Russell & Larry Wall without whom this book would not be possible.

One who plants a garden plants happiness.

If you reap what you sow,
make sure it's love
that you grow.

As in life,
few gardens
have only flowers.

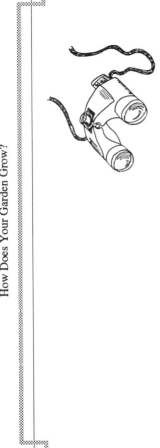

Focus on the beauty
and not on the weeds.

As we tend our garden
we nourish our soul.

Enjoy the warmth of the sun,
the coolness of the rain,
and you too
will grow and flourish.

In the garden more grows
than the gardener sows.

Plant good deeds
and you'll harvest
a rich life.

Gardens are a collaboration between art and nature.

To create a garden
is to create a better world.

You may be both
on earth and in heaven
in a garden.

What the caterpillar
calls the end,
is the beginning
for the butterfly.

Spring in the garden
is a reminder to us
of the wonder of new life!

Wildflowers
are sown by God.

There's no place
I'd rather pass the hours
than here among
the fragrant flowers.

Gardeners
build gardens to relax
then spend all their time
working in them.

When I was a child,
I played in the dirt
like a child.
When I grew up,
I played in the dirt
like a gardener.

Plants are like babies—
they know when an amateur
is handling them.

Our children
are the most important
seeds we will ever grow.

Children can be flowers or weeds depending on how we nurture their needs.

Gardening is
an exercise in optimism.

If we used gardens
to work out life's kinks,
we'd never need
to visit shrinks.

Gardening is
a person's effort
to improve his lot.

I like butterflies in my garden,
but I'd prefer
that the caterpillars
stayed at the neighbors

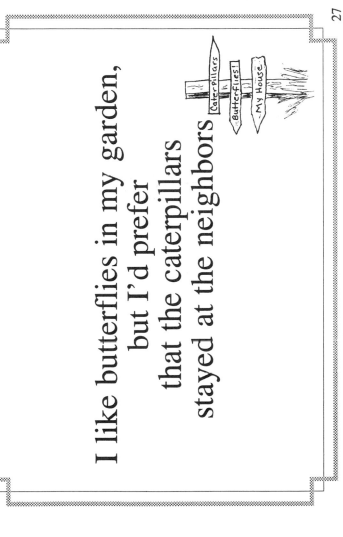

One man's garbage is
another man's compost.

You know you are
a *real* gardener
when you think compost
is a fascinating subject.

Knowledge is like manure—
it's only good
when spread around.

Plants that were
about to be removed
have a habit of suddenly
doing better.

If gardens
reflect our personality,
mine says
I'm not finished yet.

Sometimes ignorance is bliss;
you don't know enough
to see all the problems.

To spray
or not to spray,
that is the question.

When in doubt, spray.
If you can't spray
…pray!

Anyone can have dirt....
gardeners have soil.

Manure
is like a fine wine…
it gets better with age.

Gardens look better
when seen through
rose colored glasses.

Lawns are like
blind dates…
they all look good
from a distance.

A lawn reminds us that
we don't always get
what we want.

If you learn to live
with dandelions,
you'll have a perfect lawn.

Keep empty seed packages... they may come in handy for gathering the whole crop in.

May to June are good months to realize your bulbs are not coming up.

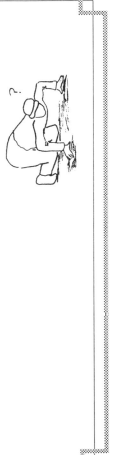

It wasn't the apple
on the tree
that ruined everything…
it was the pair
on the ground.

Forbidden fruit
is responsible
for many a bad jam.

The vegetable garden is
where the corn-fed beef dine
when the barn door is left open.

Never, Never, Never
wait just one more day
to pick a zucchini.

By the time the cost
of fertilizer, water,
and time is added up,
I figure my homegrown
tomatoes cost $10 apiece.

Manure
always smells worse
when it's in the
neighbor's yard.

Ignore what bugs you
or it might eat you up.

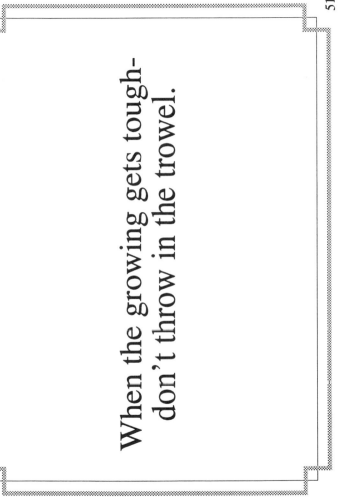

When the growing gets tough-
don't throw in the trowel.

You never promised me
a rose garden,
but a few daisies
would be nice.

Into each life
some rain must fall;
when it does,
put on big boots.

Count only sunny hours,
and dark days
will fade away.

Dreams will never die
as long as there are
garden catalogs.

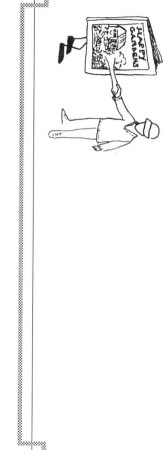

I never met a garden catalog
I didn't like.

A garden is a friend
you can visit any time.

Pull a weed,
plant some flowers.
What better way
to pass the hours.

If time is money,
gardens must be
the richest place on earth.

There are two lasting bequests
we can give our children,
roots and wings.

All the flowers
of tomorrow are in
the seeds of today.

Life began in a garden.

Bulbs are proof
that miracles happen.

Don't let lack of praise
nip you in the bud.

If you can't get the job done,
get a bigger shovel.

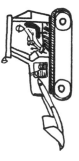

Oh woe!
when the hoe
hits your toe.

Gardeners spend half
the time on their knees
and the other half
trying to get up.

What a person
needs in gardening is
a cast-iron back
with a hinge in it.

Gardeners relax
by doing hard work.

70

How Does Your Garden Grow?

"Gardener's hands"
are a badge of honor.

Gardening is honest work
and the world needs
more honesty.

If you want to pick roses,
expect a few thorns.

Sore back, weak knees, stiff neck, darn leaves!

There's a good reason why
it's called crabgrass.

Remember when
you used to think
picking dandelions was fun?

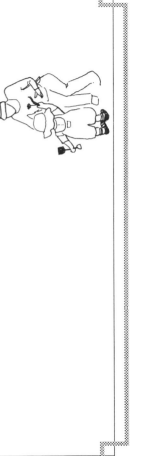

Don't believe
that "weed and feed"
is all you'll need.

A lawnmower
only starts the first time
when it's in the repair shop.

If only
we fussed over each other
as much as
we fuss over our gardens.

Gardening is like mud...
it sticks to you.

It's a Bad Garden Day
when your toddler rearranges
all the plant labels.

How Does Your Garden Grow?

It's a Bad Garden Day
when you mistake Roundup®
for Miracle-Gro®!

Miracle-Gro® is the registered trademark of Stern's Nurseries, Inc.
Roundup® is the registered trademark of Monsanto Company.

It's a Bad Garden Day
when a sack of manure
bursts open
in the trunk of your car.

It's a Bad Garden Day
when locusts
discover your address.

A vegetable garden
is a smorgasbord
for snails, slugs,
beetles and worms.

It's funny how fast snails can move through a garden.

If the early bird
catches the worm....
I'm going to sleep till noon.

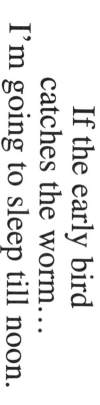

Poppies are nice...
and so are Mommies.

Garden Time Schedule:
planning...30%
planting...10%
fussing over...60%

Planning is 88% of Planting.

Whoever said,
"Life is not a Bed of Roses"
must prefer petunias.

Anyone can have nice flowers
in the Spring,
but it takes a true gardener
to have great flowers
in the Fall.

You know you are
a real gardener
when all your jeans
have holes in the knees.

Real gardeners
are down to earth.

You know you've gone
a bit overboard if
you're also planting
in the neighbor's yard.

The trouble with gardening
is that it does not
remain an avocation,
but becomes an *obsession!*

You know you are
a *real* gardener
when your plants
become your babies.

You know you are
a *real* gardener when
strangers ask for advice.

Cultivate good friends.

Out of gardens grow
fleeting flowers
but lasting friendships.

Happiness *held*
is the seed.
Happiness *shared*
is the flower.

A man of words
and not of deeds
is like a garden
full of weeds.

Hope for the future
is at the heart
of all gardening.

A garden is an act of faith.

If at first
you don't succeed,
just try another variety.

When in doubt,
pull it out.

Roses like a lot of water...
mostly "sweat."

You have to train
your roses
if you expect them
to do tricks.

Nature soon takes over
if the gardener is absent.

A meadow of wildflowers
or a sea of weeds....
depends on your
perspective.

The finest garden
is not free from weeds.

Lawns are a full time job.
Half the time you grow it,
half the time you mow it.

If you're going to grow cactus,
don't lie down on the job.

Rock gardens are nice unless your rocks keep dying.

A hot summer sun
has its advantages—
you don't have to shovel it.

Snow is great for the garden—
it covers all your mistakes.

If it's bright and sunny
after two cold and rainy days,
it's probably Monday.

You know it's going to be
a cold winter if you see
a squirrel storing Sterno®!

Sterno® is the registered trademark of Colgate–Palmolive

Dew is a big problem on lawns, especially if the neighborhood has a lot of dogs.

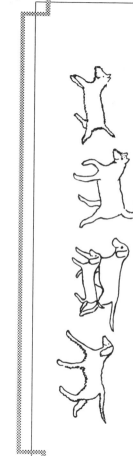

A cat's place in the garden is usually at the birdbath.

The grass may be greener
on the other side,
but you still have to mow it.

Bless all creatures here below,
except of course
the garden mole.

You know you are
a *real* gardener
if you gave up
nail polish long ago.

You know you are
a *real* gardener
when you know the importance
of digging a proper hole.

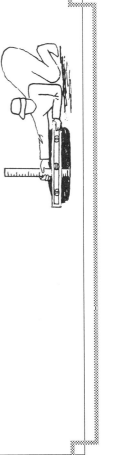

Whoever said
"Life is not a Bed of Roses"
has never visited my yard!

You know you've ordered
too much if
every time your child
sees a UPS van she shouts
"It's the rose truck!"

If April showers
bring May flowers,
can weeds be far behind?

You can't grow a pickle.

If you're a gardener,
you can always put
"plant manager"
on your resumé.

Never go to a doctor
whose office plants are dead.

Bad advice is like
too much fertilizer...
either way you'll get burned.

You're not aging...
you just need repotting.

It helps to have
"good gardening genes."

Don't forget who wears
the plants in the family.

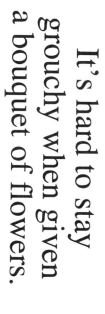

It's hard to stay grouchy when given a bouquet of flowers.

Watering is like
telling your spouse
"I love you" . . .
the more you do it,
the better the result.

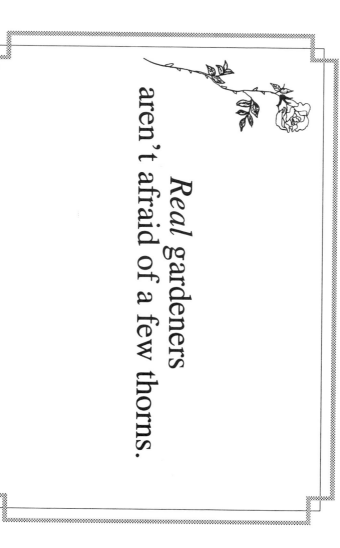

Real gardeners aren't afraid of a few thorns.

What isn't tried won't work.

A garden fills the belly
and feeds the soul.

You're still a flower
even if
you're not in the vase.

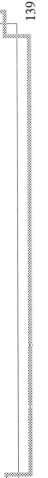

Without secure roots,
we scatter in the wind.

Be strong like a tree
that bends in the wind.

One who gardens
works hand in hand
with God.

The power that makes grass grow, fruit ripen, and guides birds in flight is in us all.

Our gardens are pockets
where our Creator keeps
our dreams.

The secrets of life
can be found in a garden.

Rejoice in Nature
as Nature rejoices
in a child.

With love,
children bloom
in the garden of life.

Weather has more meaning when you have a garden.

Garden catalogs melt
the winter snows.

Love makes us blossom.

Flowers speak
a universal language.

Share your garden with others
and you'll be surprised
how big it can grow.

Grow it with love
and you will love it.

Gardens will grow
in spite of our efforts
to improve them.

A garden is forgiving—
we get a fresh start
each spring.

Give to the earth
and it will give to you.

Plant Happiness
and it will bloom all year.

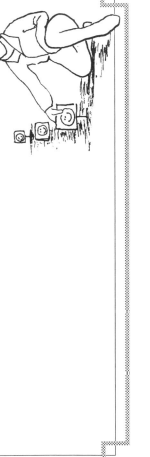

A garden grows with love.

About the Author

Beverly Rose Hopper is a Consulting Rosarian and Accredited Rose Judge for the American Rose Society. She also lectures on rose culture and has won many prestigious trophies with her roses. The author resides in San Jose, California with her husband, two young children, and 200 rosebushes.

ORDER ADDITIONAL BOOKS AS GIFTS!

HOW DOES YOUR
GARDEN GROW?   Qty _____   @ $6.95 Total _____
(ISBN # 0-963176-8-6)

ACHIEVE YOUR DREAMS   Qty _____   @ $5.95 Total _____
(ISBN # 0-963176-3-5)

MONEY
Now You Have It. Now You Don't.   Qty _____   @ $5.95 Total _____
(ISBN # 0-963176-4-3)

THE ROAD TO SUCCESS
Is Always Under Construction   Qty _____   @ $5.95 Total _____
(ISBN # 0-963176-0-0)

Add $2.00 for shipping for 1st book, 50¢ ea. thereafter _____

(Wash State residents: add applicable sales tax) _____

Send order to: Total _____

Walrus Productions	Name _____
4805 NE 106th St	Address _____
Seattle WA 98125	City/State/Zip _____

These books may be available through your local book store.